T0348851

FACE IT!

Mastering Business Finance

A PRACTICAL GUIDE TO FINANCIAL SUCCESS

SANDRO ENDLER   MBA, FMVA®, CBCA®.

ISBN: 979-8-35095-938-3

PREFACE

THIS BOOK IS FOR YOU—THE business owner who knows how important it is to manage business finance matters but feels lost about where to begin. It is for those with big dreams but struggle with understanding business finances. Whether you are starting a new business or managing an existing one, dealing with money can feel overwhelming. But in this book, you will find clear explanations, helpful advice, and practical tips just for you.

In the vast area of business books, finance topics can be tough to tackle. Business owners know they need to understand it, but sometimes have trouble finding easy-to-understand information. This book was written to fill that gap, giving you a complete yet uncomplicated guide to handling business finances.

If you are stressed out by things like balance sheets, cash flow statements, and profit margins, do not worry. This book explains financial terms in plain language and gives you the knowledge and confidence to make smart decisions for your business. Whether you want to manage cash better, get funding, or plan for growth, the explanations and tips in this book will help you find your way.

To every business owner losing sleep over money worries, remember that you are not alone. I hope this book gives you hope. Running a business is tough, but with determination and the right help, success is possible. Let this book encourage and empower you as you deal with business finances.

As you start reading, remember that knowledge is key. By learning from this book, you are taking a major step toward understanding how money works in your business. May this book light the way to financial success and prosperity for you and your business.

Get ready to boost your business smarts. Unleash your financial power and **FACE IT!**

SANDRO ENDLER

Table of Contents

INTRODUCTION:
Business Financial Management
for Small and Mid-Size Companies

"Knowledge is power. Information is liberating. Education is
the premise of progress, in every society, in every family."

KOFI ANNAN

INTRODUCTION

IN TODAY'S DYNAMIC BUSINESS ENVIRONMENT, effective financial management is vital for the success and sustainability of companies of any size, especially the small and mid-size ones. These enterprises face unique challenges and opportunities that require a strategic approach to managing their finances.

Whether navigating through periods of growth, weathering economic downturns, or capitalizing on emerging trends, understanding the fundamentals of business financial management is essential.

This introduction serves as overall information on the significance of financial management for small and midsize companies, providing an overview of key concepts essential for navigating the financial landscape.

IMPORTANCE OF FINANCIAL MANAGEMENT IN THE BUSINESS LIFECYCLE

Financial management plays a fundamental role in every stage of the business lifecycle, from inception to maturity. At the outset, entrepreneurs must carefully distribute resources and secure funding to transform their vision into a workable business venture. Sound financial planning not only helps in securing initial capital but also lays the foundation for sustainable growth.

As businesses evolve, financial management becomes increasingly important. During periods of expansion, companies must manage cash flow effectively, invest in growth opportunities, and mitigate risks associated with scaling operations. Moreover, in the expansion phase, businesses often meet challenges, such as diversification of revenue streams and geographical expansion, requiring astute financial management strategies to navigate these complexities successfully.

During economic downturns, prudent financial management can help companies weather the storm by optimizing costs, managing debt, and preserving liquidity. Implementing proper risk management practices and contingency plans enables businesses to navigate through turbulent times while keeping financial stability.

Furthermore, financial management is integral to strategic decision-making. Whether evaluating potential investments, assessing the viability of new projects, or deciding the best capital structure, informed financial analysis guides executives in making sound choices that drive long-term value creation.

Strategic financial management involves identifying and capitalizing on emerging market trends, technological advancements, and competitive opportunities to gain a competitive edge in the market.

Mastering financial management is not only about managing day-to-day transactions but also about strategically positioning the company for sustained growth and resilience across the entire business lifecycle.

By embracing sound financial principles, using advanced analytical tools, and fostering a culture of financial accountability, small- and mid-size companies can effectively navigate the complexities of the financial landscape and achieve long-term success in today's dynamic and competitive business environment.

LESSONS FROM CORPORATE FAILURES: THE PERILS OF POOR MANAGEMENT

The landscape of business is often turbulent, with success never guaranteed and failure lurking around every corner. Ten notable examples stand as reminders of the perils of poor management, each being a cautionary tale of corporate history.

Enron, once a titan of the energy industry, succumbed to the depths of bankruptcy in 2001, embroiled in a scandal of deceitful accounting practices that masked crippling debt. Similarly, the demise of **Toys R Us**, a beloved fixture of childhoods worldwide, unfolded in 2018, and its downfall was precipitated by staggering unpaid taxes.

Blockbuster, a stalwart of the video rental market, did not adapt to the digital age, filing for bankruptcy in 2010 amidst the rising dominance of online streaming platforms like Netflix. **British Home Stores (BHS)**, under the ownership of Sir Philip Green, collapsed in 2016, leaving thousands jobless and burdened with pension liabilities.

Woolworths, once a strong presence on high streets, met its downfall in 2009, succumbing to financial mismanagement and changing consumer habits.

Comet, a giant in UK electrical retail, faced a similar fate in 2012, liquidating all assets due to poor financial performance worsened by economic downturns.

Kmart's story is punctuated by repeated failures, as the company filed for bankruptcy twice.

Compaq, once a leading supplier of PC systems, faltered in the late 1990s under misguided leadership, eventually being acquired by Hewlett-Packard in 2002.

Northern Rock's collapse in 2007 marked the first British bank failure in over a century, a casualty of the global banking crisis and a catastrophic bank run.

Finally, **Lehman Brothers**, a titan of investment banking, filed for bankruptcy in 2008 with debts surpassing its assets, symbolizing the height of the financial crisis.

These examples stand as reminders of the importance of prudent management and adaptability in the face of evolving market dynamics. Their failures serve as cautionary tales for aspiring entrepreneurs and seasoned executives alike, illustrating the dire consequences of complacency and mismanagement in the unforgiving arena of business.

SMALL BUSINESSES MAY FAIL TOO. TOP REASONS FOR SMALL BUSINESS FAILURES

According to Business Insider, most small businesses fail because they run out of money, with 82 percent facing this issue. Others struggle due to not enough people wanting their product (42 percent), running out of cash (29 percent), having the wrong team (23 percent), or being outcompeted by competitors (19 percent).

Running a small business is not an easy task. I have seen many businesses fail due to money problems, like not having enough cash, forgetting to plan budgets, facing unexpected costs, having too much debt, not keeping track of finances and taxes, paying bills late, and probably the most common mistake—mixing personal and business money.

Not having enough money when needed is a common challenge for small businesses. They often face cash flow issues, meaning they may lack sufficient liquid assets to cover immediate expenses such as payroll, inventory, or equipment maintenance. These shortages can lead to disruptions in operations and missed opportunities for growth.

Another critical issue is the failure to make and stick to a budget. Budgeting is essential for small businesses to allocate resources effectively and ensure that expenses do not surpass revenue. When businesses neglect to create or adhere to a budget, they risk overspending, financial instability, and an inability to achieve long-term goals.

Preparing for unexpected expenses is vital for small businesses' financial health. They must anticipate and plan for unforeseen costs like equipment repairs, legal fees, or sudden drops in revenue. Without a contingency plan, unexpected expenses can strain finances and even threaten the business's viability.

Accumulating excessive debt is another challenge small businesses may face. Whether through loans, credit cards, or lines of credit, heavy debt burdens can lead to high-interest payments and limit financial flexibility. Additionally, substantial debt loads may make it challenging to secure additional financing or reinvest profits in the business.

Proper financial reporting is crucial for small businesses to accurately track income, expenses, and overall financial performance. Failing to report finances correctly can result in errors, compliance issues, and potentially legal consequences.

Tax compliance is essential for small businesses to meet their obligations to tax authorities. This includes filing the correct tax returns and paying taxes on time. Mistakes or negligence in tax compliance can lead to penalties, fines, and even audits.

Paying bills late can have detrimental effects on small businesses. It can damage relationships with suppliers and vendors, disrupt the supply chain, and result in higher costs due to late fees or interest charges. Consistently paying bills late can also harm the business's reputation and credibility.

Finally, mixing personal and business finances is a common mistake among small business owners. This practice can blur the lines between personal and professional assets, making it challenging to track expenses, calculate profits accurately, and obtain financing. It can also complicate tax reporting and increase the risk of legal liabilities. Therefore, it is essential to keep personal and business finances separate for financial clarity and stability.

Addressing these challenges requires initiative-taking financial management, disciplined budgeting, and adherence to best practices in accounting and taxation.

It is important to mention that small businesses may also receive help seeking professional guidance from accountants, financial advisors, or business mentors to navigate these issues effectively. It is worth the investment in professional guidance to help you implement key financial concepts in your business.

LOOKING TO WHAT MATTERS MOST: OVERVIEW OF KEY FINANCIAL CONCEPTS

A solid grasp of key financial concepts is essential for small and midsize companies to make informed decisions and achieve their strategic goals. Some of the fundamental concepts are described below and will be addressed in depth in this book:

- **Budgeting and Forecasting:** Financial planning involves setting goals, finding resources, and developing strategies to achieve organizational goals. Forecasting, on the other hand, entails predicting future financial outcomes based on historical data and market trends, enabling companies to expect challenges and capitalize on opportunities.

- **Accounts Receivable, Accounts Payable and Cost Control:** Budgeting is the process of distributing financial resources to various activities within the organization, ensuring alignment with strategic priorities. Cost control measures aim to minimize expenses without compromising quality or efficiency, thereby enhancing profitability and sustainability.

- **Cash Flow Management:** Effective cash flow management involves checking the inflow and outflow of cash to ensure liquidity and meet financial obligations. By perfecting cash flow cycles, companies can enhance their financial flexibility and seize growth opportunities as they arise.

- **Capital Budgeting and Investment Analysis:** Capital budgeting involves evaluating potential investment opportunities and finding their feasibility in terms of risk and return. By employing techniques such as net present value (NPV) analysis and internal rate of return (IRR), companies can prioritize projects that generate the highest value for shareholders.

- **Financial Risk Management:** Financial risk arises from uncertainties in the economic environment, market conditions, and business operations. Risk management strategies help companies mitigate potential losses and protect their financial stability.

CONCLUSION

Understanding the importance of financial management and mastering key financial concepts are indispensable for small and midsize companies striving for success in today's competitive landscape. By adopting a strategic approach to financial management, businesses can enhance their resilience, optimize performance, and unlock sustainable growth opportunities.

In essence, financial management is more than daily transactions; it is about strategically positioning a company for growth and resilience through every phase of its lifecycle. By adopting solid financial principles and using reliable analytical reports, small- and mid-size companies can thrive in today's dynamic business environment.

CHAPTER 1:
Budgeting and Forecasting - The Compass of Your Business

"If you don't know where you are going,
any road will get you there"

LEWIS CARROLL

NAVIGATING WITHOUT A COMPASS CAN lead to aimless direction, missed opportunities, and even disaster. Just as a ship relies on its compass to chart a course through turbulent waters, businesses depend on financial planning and forecasting to position them toward success. In this chapter, we will dig into two crucial aspects of business financial management: budgeting and forecasting, likening them to the compass of your business.

BUDGETING AND FORECASTING – THE BUSINESS COMPASS

Imagine you are embarking on a journey across an untraveled territory. Before setting sail, you would meticulously plan your route, anticipate challenges, and allocate resources accordingly. Similarly, **budgeting and forecasting** serve as the compass of your business, guiding your financial decisions and ensuring you stay on course toward your goals.

BUDGETING

It involves setting financial targets for your business over a specified period, typically a fiscal year. It is a process that requires careful consideration of revenue projections, expenses, and investment needs. By setting up a budget, you create a roadmap for distributing resources efficiently, finding areas for cost savings, and prioritizing strategic initiatives.

It is a fundamental financial management practice that plays a crucial role in the success and sustainability of any business, organization, or individual's financial health. It involves the systematic process of planning and allocating financial resources over a defined period, usually a fiscal year, to achieve specific objectives and goals.

Budgeting is a practice that should not be taken lightly; actually, it should be taken as a top priority for the benefit of the business.

Here is a deeper exploration of the components and significance of budgeting:

Financial Targets and Goals: Budgeting begins with establishing clear financial targets and goals for the business. These objectives may include revenue growth, cost reduction, profit margins, market expansion, investment in new ventures, or debt reduction. Defining these targets provides a framework for the budgeting process and aligns financial decisions with the overall strategic direction of the business.

Revenue Projections: One of the primary elements of budgeting is forecasting and estimating revenue streams. This involves analyzing historical sales data, market trends, customer behavior, and other relevant factors to predict future income. Accurate revenue projections serve as the foundation for setting realistic financial goals and determining the resources available for expenditure.

Expense Allocation: Budgeting requires a thorough examination and allocation of resources to various expense categories. These may include operational costs such as rent, utilities, payroll, inventory, marketing, research and development, and administrative expenses. By categorizing and allocating expenses based on their importance and necessity, businesses can ensure efficient resource utilization and avoid overspending in areas that do not contribute to their strategic objectives.

Investment Needs: Budgeting also includes identifying investment opportunities and allocating funds for capital expenditures, expansion projects, technology upgrades, and other initiatives aimed at enhancing long-term growth and competitiveness. By prioritizing investments based on their potential return on investment (ROI) and strategic significance, businesses can allocate resources effectively to drive sustainable growth and innovation.

Resource Allocation and Optimization: A well-designed budget serves as a roadmap for resource allocation, enabling businesses to optimize their financial resources and prioritize initiatives that deliver the highest value. By identifying areas for cost savings, streamlining processes, and eliminating inefficiencies, budgeting helps businesses maximize profitability and operational performance.

Monitoring and Control: Budgeting is not a one-time exercise but an ongoing process that requires regular monitoring, review, and adjustment. Businesses must track their actual financial performance against budgeted targets, identify variances, and take corrective actions as needed to ensure alignment with strategic objectives. By maintaining financial discipline and accountability, budgeting enables businesses to stay agile and responsive to changing market conditions and emerging opportunities.

Budgeting is a dynamic and integral aspect of financial management that enables businesses to plan, allocate, and optimize financial resources effectively to achieve their strategic objectives and drive sustainable growth and profitability.

By setting clear financial targets, projecting revenues, allocating expenses, prioritizing investments, and monitoring performance, businesses can navigate economic uncertainties and position themselves for long-term success in a competitive marketplace. **Budgeting is a must-have.**

FORECASTING

It is about predicting future financial performance based on historical data, market trends, and internal factors. While budgeting sets the framework for financial planning, forecasting provides insights into potential outcomes and helps you adapt to changing circumstances. Whether it is anticipating fluctuations in demand, adjusting production schedules, or evaluating the impact of external factors, accurate forecasting enables decision-making and risk management.

Forecasting in financial management is a critical process that involves predicting future financial performance based on various inputs, such as historical data, market trends, and internal factors. It serves as a strategic tool to anticipate potential outcomes, assist in decision-making, and risk management.

Here is a more detailed exploration of key aspects:

Data Analysis and Historical Trends: Forecasting begins with a comprehensive analysis of historical financial data. By examining past performance, trends, and patterns, financial analysts can identify key indicators that may influence future outcomes. This analysis may encompass sales figures, revenue streams, expenses, market conditions, and other relevant metrics.

Market Trends and External Factors: In addition to internal data, forecasting also considers external factors that could impact financial performance. These may include changes in consumer behavior, shifts in market demand, economic conditions, regulatory changes, technological advancements, and geopolitical events. By staying attuned to these external variables, organizations can better anticipate potential opportunities and threats.

Scenario Planning and Sensitivity Analysis: Forecasting involves creating multiple scenarios or models to account for different potential outcomes. This may include best-case, worst-case, and most likely scenarios. Sensitivity analysis helps assess the impact of changes in key variables on financial projections. By considering various scenarios, organizations can better prepare for uncertainty and make informed decisions.

Resource Allocation and Planning: Accurate forecasting enables organizations to allocate resources effectively and plan for future investments. Whether it is allocating budgets for marketing campaigns, R&D projects, or capital expenditures, forecasting provides valuable insights into resource requirements and potential returns on investment. This ensures that resources are allocated efficiently to support strategic objectives.

Performance Monitoring and Course Correction: Once forecasts are in place, it is essential to monitor actual performance against predicted outcomes. Regular performance reviews help identify deviations from the forecast and enable timely course corrections. This may involve adjusting strategies, reallocating resources, or implementing contingency plans to mitigate risks and capitalize on opportunities.

Communication and Stakeholder Engagement: Forecasting involves collaboration across various departments and stakeholders within an organization. Effective communication of financial forecasts and assumptions is crucial for aligning stakeholders around common goals and objectives. By fostering transparency and accountability, organizations can build trust and confidence in their financial planning processes.

Continuous Improvement and Adaptation: Financial forecasting is not a one-time exercise but an ongoing process that requires continuous refinement and adaptation. As market conditions evolve and new information becomes available, forecasts may need to be adjusted accordingly. By embracing a culture of continuous improvement, organizations can enhance the accuracy and reliability of their forecasts over time.

In conclusion, forecasting plays a vital role in financial management by providing insights into potential outcomes, facilitating decision-making, and enabling proactive risk management. By leveraging historical data, market trends, and scenario analysis, organizations can anticipate changes, allocate resources effectively, and navigate uncertain environments with greater confidence.

Together, budgeting and forecasting form the cornerstone of effective financial planning, providing clarity and direction amidst uncertainty. By continuously checking performance against budgeted targets and refining forecasts, businesses can course-correct as needed, ensuring they stay agile and responsive in dynamic markets.

EXPANDING HORIZONS: INTEGRATING BUDGETING AND FORECASTING WITH THE FINANCIAL STATEMENTS

The constructive interaction between budgeting and forecasting, and financial statement analysis becomes apparent when these practices are integrated into a company's strategic planning process. By aligning financial goals with operational objectives, businesses can gear the full potential of financial planning to drive performance and achieve long-term success.

Integration begins with a comprehensive understanding of the business environment, including market dynamics, competitive pressures, and regulatory requirements. By conducting a thorough analysis of internal and external factors, businesses can find opportunities for growth, anticipate threats, and develop strategies to capitalize on their strengths.

With a clear understanding of their competitive landscape and market positioning, businesses can set realistic financial targets and develop actionable plans to achieve them. Budgeting provides a framework for distributing resources effectively, while forecasting enables businesses to anticipate changes in market conditions and adjust their strategies accordingly.

Financial statement analysis plays a crucial role in monitoring performance against established goals, finding deviations from expected outcomes, and implementing corrective measures as needed. By conducting regular reviews of financial statements, businesses can track progress, evaluate the effectiveness of their strategies, and make informed decisions to drive continuous improvement. We will be covering the Financial Statements topic in Chapter 8 of this book.

Moreover, integrating financial planning into the strategic planning process fosters collaboration across functional areas within the organization. By involving key stakeholders in the decision-making process, businesses can use diverse perspectives, align goals, and foster a culture of accountability and transparency.

The integration of these two processes empowers businesses to make informed decisions, mitigate risks, and seize opportunities for growth. By using the compass of financial planning and analysis, businesses can navigate the complexities of the business landscape with confidence, setting a course toward sustainable success.

CONCLUSION

Budgeting and Forecasting is a detailed guide that shows how important it is for businesses to plan and predict their finances well. It explains that budgeting and forecasting are not just tools for navigation but also help businesses see where they are headed financially.

By carefully looking at budgeting and forecasting, it can be understood how they help businesses foresee and handle risks, take advantage of opportunities, and use resources well. Planning carefully helps businesses anticipate problems, adapt to changes in the market quickly, and make the most of new trends, which makes them stronger and more competitive.

When budgeting and forecasting are part of the big picture strategy, businesses can be more flexible, innovative, and grow sustainably.

In summary, budgeting and forecasting are not just routine tasks—they are key to a business's success. When businesses are good at budgeting and forecasting, they can manage the challenges of today's market confidently and plan for a future of growth and success.

CHAPTER 2:

Accounts Receivable, Accounts Payable, and Cost Control - Controlling the Faucet.

"Watch the costs and the profits will take care of themselves."

—ANDREW CARNEGIE

I OFTEN SAY TO PEOPLE THAT come to me to discuss cost controls that: **"when the tide recedes, the rocks appear."** In other words, it is a critical reality: attention to costs and expenses usually is neglected in times of high revenue; on the other hand, during times of financial constraint and diminished revenue, everybody starts to pay attention to unnecessary costs and expenses.

In business financial management, effective management of accounts receivable (A/R), accounts payable (A/P), and cost control are fundamental aspects that significantly influence a company's financial health and success.

This chapter targets cost control, accounts payable, and accounts receivable. Through examining these components, businesses can adeptly manage their financial outflows and inflows, ensuring operational resilience.

By developing strategies for effective cost management and optimizing the processes for handling payments made and received, companies are better equipped to navigate financial downturns and capitalize on periods of growth, enhancing over-all profitability.

ACCOUNTS RECEIVABLE MANAGEMENT

Accounts receivable represent the amounts owed to a company by its customers for goods or services delivered on credit. While extending credit can boost sales and foster customer relation-ships, it also introduces the risk of delayed or defaulted payments, which can strain cash flow and impede business operations. Therefore, efficient management of A/R is essential for main-taining liquidity and mitigating financial risks.

1. Establishing Credit Policies

The first step in effective A/R management is to establish clear and consistent credit policies. These policies should outline the criteria for extending credit to customers, including creditwor-thiness assessments, credit limits, payment terms, and procedures for handling delinquent accounts. By defining these parameters upfront, companies can minimize the likelihood of bad debts and ensure timely collections.

2. Credit Analysis

Conducting a thorough credit analysis is crucial to assessing the creditworthiness of customers and mitigating the risk of non-payment. This involves evaluating factors such as the cus-tomer's financial stability, payment history, industry trends, and economic conditions. By using credit scoring models and credit reports, companies can make informed decisions regarding credit approval and determine appropriate credit terms.

3. Invoicing and Billing

Efficient invoicing and billing processes are essential for prompt payment collection and accurate accounting. Companies should strive to generate invoices promptly upon delivering goods or services, ensuring clarity regarding payment terms, due dates, and accepted payment methods. Leveraging electronic invoicing systems can streamline the billing process, reduce errors, and expedite payment processing.

4. Monitoring and Collections

Regular monitoring of accounts receivable is critical to identifying overdue payments and proactively addressing collection issues. Companies should implement robust collection procedures, including reminders, statements, and follow-up communications, to encourage timely payment from customers. Automated collection tools and software can help streamline this process and improve collection efficiency.

5. Cash Flow Forecasting

Effective A/R management involves forecasting cash flow to anticipate future inflows accurately. By analyzing historical payment patterns, sales forecasts, and customer payment behavior, companies can develop reliable cash flow projections to inform budgeting and financial planning decisions. This enables the management of working capital and ensures sufficient liquidity to meet operational needs.

ACCOUNTS PAYABLE MANAGEMENT

Accounts payable are the amounts owed by a company to its suppliers and vendors for goods or services received on credit. Efficient management of A/P is essential for optimizing cash flow, maintaining positive supplier relationships, and maximizing available discounts.

1. Vendor Selection and Negotiation

Strategic vendor selection and negotiation play a crucial role in A/P management. Companies should assess vendor performance, reliability, and pricing to identify preferred suppliers that offer competitive terms and quality products or services. Negotiating favorable payment terms, discounts for advance payment, and volume-based discounts can help optimize A/P and enhance profitability.

2. Invoice Processing and Approval

Streamlining invoice processing and approval workflows is essential for timely payment and accurate financial reporting. Companies should implement efficient procedures for receiving, reviewing, and approving invoices, ensuring proper verification of goods or services received and adherence to contractual terms. Automated invoice processing systems can expedite this process, reduce errors, and enhance control over A/P functions.

3. Cash Management and Payment Optimization

Optimizing cash management practices is crucial for managing A/P effectively and maximizing available discounts. Companies should leverage cash flow forecasting tools to prioritize payments based on due dates, cash availability, and potential discount opportunities. Adopting electronic payment methods, such as automated clearing house (ACH) transfers or electronic funds transfers (EFT), can accelerate payment processing and streamline reconciliation processes.

4. Vendor Relationship Management

Building strong relationships with vendors is essential for fostering collaboration, resolving disputes, and negotiating favorable terms. Regular communication, transparency, and timely payment demonstrate reliability and trustworthiness, which can lead to preferential treatment and mutually beneficial partnerships. Implementing vendor performance metrics and feedback mechanisms can facilitate continuous improvement and accountability in vendor relationships.

COST CONTROL STRATEGIES

Cost control is a fundamental aspect of business financial management aimed at optimizing expenses while maximizing value creation and profitability. By implementing effective cost control strategies, companies can identify cost-saving opportunities, improve operational efficiency, and enhance competitiveness in the marketplace.

1. Cost Analysis and Budgeting

Conducting comprehensive cost analysis and budgeting is essential for identifying cost drivers, evaluating spending patterns, and establishing cost-saving targets. Companies should scrutinize expenses across all areas of operations, including production, marketing, and overhead, to identify inefficiencies and areas for optimization. Developing detailed budgets and variance analysis reports enables cost management and accountability.

2. Process Improvement

Adopting continuous process improvement methodologies can drive cost efficiencies and enhance productivity. Companies should streamline workflows, eliminate waste, and standardize processes to reduce cycle times, minimize inventory levels, and lower production costs. Implementing technologies such as automation, robotics, and data analytics can further optimize operations and resource utilization.

3. Strategic Sourcing and Vendor Management

Strategic sourcing involves identifying reliable suppliers, negotiating favorable terms, and optimizing procurement processes to minimize costs and maximize value. Companies should evaluate supplier performance, assess market dynamics, and leverage economies of scale to achieve cost savings through bulk purchasing, supplier consolidation, and contract renegotiation. Effective vendor management practices, such as supplier scorecards and performance reviews, ensure alignment with business objectives and mitigate supply chain risks.

4. Cost-Reduction Initiatives

Implementing targeted cost reduction initiatives can yield significant savings and improve financial performance. Companies should engage employees at all levels to identify cost-saving opportunities, encourage innovation, and foster a culture of cost consciousness. This may involve restructuring operations, outsourcing non-core activities, renegotiating contracts, or reevaluating overhead expenses to eliminate redundancies and inefficiencies.

CONCLUSION

In this chapter, we have explored the critical components of accounts receivable (A/R), accounts payable (A/P), and cost control, explaining their impact on a company's financial health and sustainability. Through the lens of effective management in these areas, businesses can navigate the complexities of financial operations with agility and foresight.

Mastering accounts receivable, accounts payable, and cost control is fundamental to controlling the faucet of financial flows within a company. By diligently managing these facets, businesses can weather economic fluctuations, capitalize on growth opportunities, and achieve sustained success in today's dynamic business landscape.

Effective management of accounts receivable, accounts payable, and cost control is essential for achieving financial stability, operational efficiency, and sustainable growth in today's competitive business environment.

By implementing sound financial practices, leveraging technology, and fostering collaborative relationships with stakeholders, companies can optimize cash flow, minimize risks, and enhance shareholder value, positioning themselves for long-term success.

CHAPTER 3:

Cash Flow Management – Controlling the heartbeat of the business.

"If I had to run a company on three measures, those measures would be customer satisfaction, employee satisfaction and cash flow."

JACK WELCH

FIRST THINGS FIRST: **C**ASH IS **king!** It holds unparalleled importance in business operations. To enhance it, a comprehensive understanding of operational cash flow is essential.

Cash flow management is a critical component of business financial management, focusing on the effective monitoring, analysis, and optimization of cash inflows and outflows within an organization. A robust cash flow management strategy enables companies to maintain liquidity, meet financial obligations, invest in growth opportunities, and navigate economic uncertainties.

In this chapter, we get into the principles, strategies, and best practices of cash flow management, equipping businesses with the tools and insights necessary to enhance their financial resilience and success.

IMPORTANCE OF CASH FLOW MANAGEMENT

When working with my clients, I always make sure to start by checking out the client's operational cash flow report. Having worked in business financial management for quite some time, I have found that this report holds an irreplaceable function of essential information. It is like the key to understanding how well a company is doing financially and how smoothly its operations are running. By focusing on this report first, I aim to get a clear picture of where the company stands financially and help them make smart decisions for the future.

Having said that, I can say with confidence that effective cash flow management is vital for sustaining business operations, supporting growth initiatives, and safeguarding against financial distress. By maintaining adequate liquidity and cash reserves, companies can weather economic downturns, seize strategic opportunities, and maintain the confidence of stakeholders, including creditors, investors, and employees.

Some key benefits of robust cash flow management include the following:

Liquidity Management: Ensuring sufficient cash reserves to meet short-term obligations, such as payroll, rent, and supplier payments, reduces the risk of insolvency and enhances financial stability.

Working Capital Optimization: Managing working capital effectively involves balancing the timing of cash inflows and outflows associated with inventory, accounts receivable, and accounts payable to minimize financing costs and maximize operational efficiency.

Investment and Growth Opportunities: Positive cash flow enables companies to reinvest in their business, fund expansion initiatives, and pursue strategic acquisitions or investments that drive long-term value creation.

Risk Mitigation: Initiative-taking cash flow management helps identify and mitigate financial risks, such as cash flow volatility, liquidity constraints, and debt repayment obligations, minimizing the likelihood of default or financial distress.

UNDERSTANDING AND BUILDING STRATEGIES FOR CASH FLOW MANAGEMENT

Cash flow refers to the movement of cash into and out of a business over a specific period, typically measured monthly, quarterly, or annually. Positive cash flow occurs when cash inflows exceed cash outflows, indicating that a company has sufficient funds to cover its expenses and obligations. Conversely, negative cash flow occurs when outflows exceed inflows, necessitating the use of cash reserves or external financing to bridge the shortfall.

To enhance cash flow management effectiveness, businesses can implement a range of strategies and best practices tailored to their unique circumstances and objectives. Key strategies include:

1. Cash Flow Forecasting

Developing accurate cash flow forecasts is a cornerstone of effective cash flow management, providing visibility into future cash inflows and outflows and enabling decision-making. Companies should utilize historical data, sales projections, and budget assumptions to create comprehensive cash flow projections for various time horizons. Regular monitoring and updating of forecasts allow businesses to anticipate cash flow fluctuations, identify potential liquidity gaps, and implement preemptive measures to address them.

2. Working Capital Optimization

Optimizing working capital involves managing the cash conversion cycle—the time it takes to convert inventory and receivables into cash and payables into payments. Companies can reduce the cash tied up in working capital by negotiating favorable payment terms with suppliers to extend payment deadlines without incurring penalties. Implementing efficient inventory management practices, such as just-in-time (JIT) inventory systems, to minimize excess inventory and carrying costs. Accelerating accounts receivable collections through prompt invoicing, initiative-taking follow-up, and offering incentives for advance payment.

By streamlining working capital processes, companies can improve cash flow efficiency and free up funds for other business priorities.

3. Expense Management

Controlling expenses is essential for preserving cash flow and maintaining profitability, particularly during periods of economic uncertainty or market volatility. Companies should conduct regular expense reviews to identify cost-saving opportunities, eliminate non-essential expenditures, and negotiate favorable terms with vendors and service providers. Implementing cost control measures across all areas of operations, including overhead, marketing, and administrative expenses, helps optimize cash flow and enhance financial resilience.

4. Cash Flow Enhancement Strategies

In addition to cost reduction initiatives, businesses can explore various strategies to enhance cash flow by offering discounts for advance payments to incentivize prompt customer settlements and improve cash flow predictability. Implementing cash management techniques, such as cash pooling, to consolidate cash balances across multiple accounts and optimize liquidity management. Exploring alternative financing options, such as lines of credit, factoring, or asset-based lending, to supplement working capital and bridge short-term cash flow gaps.

By adopting cash flow enhancement strategies, companies can bolster their financial flexibility and mitigate the impact of cash flow fluctuations on business operations.

5. Capital Expenditure Management

Prudent management of capital expenditures is essential for aligning investment decisions with cash flow objectives and maximizing return on investment. Companies should prioritize capital projects based on their strategic importance, potential financial returns, and available funding sources. Conducting thorough cost-benefit analyses, assessing project risks, and evaluating alternative financing options help ensure that capital expenditures are in line with cash flow constraints and long-term business objectives.

CONCLUSION

In conclusion, mastering the art of cash flow management is absolutely vital for businesses to not just survive but thrive in today's constantly evolving business landscape. It is like monitoring the heartbeat of a company's financial health, supporting its growth, and ensuring it can weather any storm that comes its way.

By adopting effective cash flow strategies such as forecasting, carefully monitoring expenses, optimizing how money flows in and out of the business, and paying close attention to operational cash flow reports, companies can ensure they always have enough money to keep things running smoothly.

It is crucial not to overlook the importance of tracking operational cash flow—essentially, tracking the day-to-day ins and outs of money within the company. This gives businesses a clear picture of their financial health and helps them make informed decisions to avoid potential cash crunches or financial pitfalls.

These steps are not just about keeping the lights on; they are about creating value for everyone involved—from employees to investors. By staying on top of cash flow management, businesses can build resilience, minimize risks, and continue to grow, even in the face of uncertainty. So, as markets shift and challenges arise, one thing remains clear: effective cash flow management is not just a clever idea—it is vital for lasting success in the business world.

CHAPTER 4:
Capital Budgeting and Investment Analysis

"Predicting rain doesn't count, building the ark does."

WARREN BUFFET

IMAGINE YOU ARE AN ENTREPRENEUR navigating the complex seas of business finance. Picture yourself charting a course toward success amidst uncertain waters. In your journey, you come across a timeless wisdom from none other than Warren Buffet: "Predicting rain doesn't count; building the ark does." This simple yet profound quote encapsulates the essence of capital budgeting and investment analysis—it is not enough to foresee challenges; what truly matters is taking decisive action to navigate them.

Now, let us break it down: Capital budgeting and investment analysis are not just fancy terms; they are the map guiding your business through the financial landscape. They are about making smart choices regarding where to invest your hard-earned resources for the long haul. It is like being the captain of a ship, carefully weighing the risks and rewards of different routes before setting sail.

Capital budgeting and investment analysis are integral processes within business financial management, guiding decision-making regarding long-term investments in projects, assets, and business ventures. Effective capital budgeting entails evaluating the potential returns and risks associated with investment opportunities to allocate financial resources strategically and maximize shareholder value.

In this chapter, we explore the principles, methodologies, and best practices of capital budgeting and investment analysis, empowering businesses to make informed investment decisions that drive sustainable growth and profitability.

UNDERSTANDING CAPITAL BUDGETING

Capital budgeting involves assessing and selecting investment projects that require substantial financial outlays and have long-term implications for the company's operations and financial performance. These investments typically include acquisitions, expansions, new product developments, infrastructure upgrades, and other strategic initiatives aimed at generating future cash flows and enhancing competitive advantage. Do not underestimate that. It is crucial to make sound investment decisions for your business.

IMPORTANCE OF CAPITAL BUDGETING

Capital budgeting plays a fundamental role in business financial management.

Resource Allocation: Capital budgeting enables companies to allocate limited financial resources efficiently to projects with the highest potential for value creation, ensuring optimal use of capital and maximizing returns.

Strategic Planning: By evaluating investment opportunities in the context of the company's strategic objectives and market dynamics, capital budgeting informs strategic planning initiatives and guides resource allocation decisions aligned with long-term business goals.

Risk Management: Through rigorous analysis and risk assessment, capital budgeting helps identify and mitigate investment risks, ensuring that projects are chosen with a clear understanding of potential challenges and uncertainties.

Performance Evaluation: Capital budgeting facilitates the evaluation of investment performance against predetermined benchmarks and targets, enabling companies to assess the effectiveness of capital allocation decisions and adjust strategies accordingly.

CAPITAL BUDGETING TECHNIQUES

Several techniques and methodologies can be employed in capital budgeting to evaluate investment opportunities and assess their financial viability. In this chapter, I am mentioning the three most basic ones. Each approach offers unique insights into the investment's potential returns, risks, and impact on shareholder value.

These three key capital budgeting methodologies are **quantitative techniques**:

1. Net Present Value (NPV)

Net present value (NPV) analysis assesses the present value of an investment's expected cash flows by discounting them back to their present value using a predetermined discount rate, typically the company's cost of capital. The NPV represents the difference between the present value of cash inflows and outflows associated with the investment. A positive NPV indicates that the investment is expected to generate returns exceeding the cost of capital and is therefore considered financially viable.

2. Internal Rate of Return (IRR)

The internal rate of return (IRR) is the discount rate at which the NPV of an investment equals zero, representing the rate of return at which the investment breaks even. The IRR provides insights into the investment's profitability and compares it with the company's cost of capital. A higher IRR suggests greater profitability, while a lower IRR may indicate higher risk or lower expected returns.

3. Payback Period

The payback period measures the time required for an investment to recoup its initial cost through expected cash inflows. Investments with shorter payback periods are generally preferred as they offer faster returns and lower risk of capital tied up in the project. However, the payback period does not account for the time value of money or cash flows beyond the payback period, making it less robust for evaluating long-term investments.

INVESTMENT ANALYSIS FRAMEWORK

In addition to quantitative techniques, investment analysis involves qualitative considerations and risk assessment to evaluate the broader impact and feasibility of investment opportunities.

A comprehensive investment analysis framework with a **qualitative** approach typically includes the following components:

1. Market Analysis

Conducting market analysis involves assessing the demand for the product or service offered by the investment project, analyzing market trends, competitive dynamics, and regulatory factors that may affect its success. Understanding the market environment helps gauge the potential market share, pricing dynamics, and revenue projections for the investment.

2. Financial Analysis

Financial analysis evaluates the financial feasibility and performance metrics of the investment project, including revenue projections, cost estimates, profitability margins, and cash flow forecasts. Key financial metrics such as return on investment (ROI), return on equity (ROE), and operating margins provide insights into the project's financial viability and potential for value creation.

3. Risk Assessment

Identifying and assessing investment risks is essential for mitigating potential challenges and uncertainties that may impact the success of the project. Risks may include market risks, operational risks, regulatory risks, financial risks, and external factors such as economic conditions or geopolitical events. Implementing risk management strategies and contingency plans helps minimize the impact of adverse events and enhance the project's resilience.

4. Strategic Alignment

Aligning investment decisions with the company's strategic objectives and long-term vision is crucial for ensuring coherence and constructive interaction across the organization. Investments should complement existing business operations, leverage core competencies, and contribute to sustainable growth and competitive advantage. Strategic alignment enhances the likelihood of successful implementation and maximizes the overall impact of investment initiatives.

CONCLUSION

In conclusion, capital budgeting and investment analysis are indispensable processes within business financial management, guiding strategic decision-making and resource allocation to maximize shareholder value and achieve long-term growth objectives.

Throughout this chapter, we have looked at many tools for making these decisions, like NPV (net present value), IRR (internal rate of return), and others. These tools help businesses figure out if an investment is worth it by comparing how much money they will make in the future to how much they have to spend now.

But it is not just about numbers. We have also talked about looking at the bigger picture—things like understanding the market, looking at risks, and making sure investments fit with the company's goals.

By using all of these tools and insights, companies can make better decisions about where to put their money. Decisions that not only help them grow and make money but also keep them ahead of the competition.

So, as we finish this chapter, let us remember that capital budgeting and investment analysis are not just tasks—they are super important strategies for making sure companies thrive financially.

CHAPTER 5:

Risk Management –
Avoiding the unknown.

"Risk is a function of how poorly a strategy will
perform if the 'wrong' scenario occurs."

MICHAEL PORTER

IN TODAY'S DYNAMIC BUSINESS ENVIRONMENT characterized
by volatility, uncertainty, complexity, and ambiguity, effective
risk management is essential for safeguarding against potential
threats, maximizing opportunities, and enhancing shareholder
value.

Risk management is a fundamental aspect of business
financial management, encompassing the identification, assessment, mitigation, and monitoring of risks that may impact a
company's objectives, operations, and financial performance.

In this chapter, we explore the principles, strategies, and
best practices of risk management, equipping businesses with
the tools and insights necessary to navigate risks effectively and
achieve sustainable success.

UNDERSTANDING RISK MANAGEMENT

Risk management involves the systematic process of identifying,
assessing, prioritizing, and responding to risks that may affect the
achievement of organizational objectives. Risks can arise from

various sources, including internal factors such as operational processes, strategic decisions, and human resources, as well as external factors such as market dynamics, regulatory changes, technological disruptions, and geopolitical events.

IMPORTANCE OF RISK MANAGEMENT

Effective risk management is critical for numerous reasons:

Preserving Value: By identifying and mitigating risks that may impact the company's financial performance, reputation, or stakeholder relationships, risk management helps preserve shareholder value and safeguard long-term sustainability.

Enhancing Resilience: Risk management strengthens the company's resilience to external shocks, uncertainties, and disruptions, enabling it to withstand adverse events and emerge stronger from challenging situations.

Supporting Decision-Making: Risk management provides decision-makers with valuable insights into potential risks and uncertainties associated with strategic initiatives, investments, and business operations, facilitating informed decision-making and risk-aware behavior.

Compliance and Governance: Effective risk management practices ensure compliance with regulatory requirements, industry standards, and corporate governance principles, reducing the risk of legal liabilities, fines, and reputational damage.

RISK MANAGEMENT PROCESS

The risk management process typically consists of the following steps:

1. Risk Identification

The first step in risk management involves identifying and understanding potential risks that may affect the organization's objectives and operations. This involves conducting risk assessments, brainstorming sessions, scenario analysis, and utilizing historical data and industry benchmarks to identify both internal and external risks across various areas of the business.

2. Risk Assessment

Once risks have been identified, they are assessed in terms of their likelihood of occurrence, potential impact, and significance to the organization. Risk assessment techniques such as qualitative assessment (using risk matrices or scoring criteria) and quantitative analysis (using probabilistic models) help prioritize risks based on their severity and likelihood, enabling companies to focus resources on the most critical areas.

3. Risk Mitigation

After assessing risks, companies develop and implement risk mitigation strategies to reduce the likelihood or impact of identified risks. Mitigation measures may include implementing internal controls, process improvements, risk transfer mechanisms (such as insurance), diversification strategies, contingency planning, and crisis management protocols. The goal is to minimize the residual risk exposure to an acceptable level while balancing risk and reward considerations.

4. Risk Monitoring and Review

Risk management requires dynamic monitoring, review, and action adapted to changing circumstances. Companies establish risk monitoring mechanisms, such as key risk indicators (KRIs), dashboards, and regular risk reporting, to track the effectiveness of risk mitigation measures and identify emerging risks or trends. Regular risk reviews and audits ensure that risk management practices remain aligned with organizational objectives and regulatory requirements.

TYPES OF RISKS

Risk management encompasses distinct types of risks that may impact various aspects of the business. Common categories of risks include:

- **Operational Risks**
Operational risks arise from internal processes, systems, people, or external events that may disrupt business operations, result in financial losses, or damage the company's reputation. Examples include operational failures, supply chain disruptions, human errors, cybersecurity threats, and regulatory non-compliance.

- **Financial Risks**
Financial risks pertain to uncertainties related to the company's financial position, cash flow, and capital structure. Examples include market risks (such as interest rate risk, foreign exchange

risk, and commodity price risk), credit risks (default risk associated with counterparties or customers), liquidity risks, and capital adequacy risks.

- **Strategic Risks**

    Strategic risks arise from strategic decisions, competitive dynamics, market trends, and changes in industry or regulatory environments that may impact the company's ability to achieve its strategic objectives. Examples include market entry risks, competitive threats, technological disruptions, and geopolitical uncertainties.

- **Compliance and Regulatory Risks**

Non-compliance with laws, regulations, industry standards, or internal policies can lead to compliance and regulatory risks. These risks can result in legal liabilities, fines, harm to reputation, and missed business opportunities for the company. Examples include regulatory changes, data privacy breaches, anti-money laundering violations, and environmental compliance risks.

CONCLUSION

It is crucial to underscore the indispensable role of risk management within business financial management. Risk management serves as the guardian of a company's stability and growth, acting as a vigilant sentinel against the myriad threats lurking in the business landscape.

Through diligent identification, thorough assessment, proactive mitigation, and continuous monitoring of risks, companies can shield themselves from potential pitfalls that may impede their progress. Whether it is regulatory changes, market fluctuations, operational disruptions, or unforeseen crises, a robust risk management framework equips businesses with the foresight and agility needed to navigate turbulent waters.

Effective risk management is not just about defense; it is also about offense. By embracing risk intelligently, companies can capitalize on opportunities that others may overlook, leveraging their risk awareness as a competitive advantage.

In today's dynamic and uncertain environment, the importance of effective risk management cannot be overstated. It is not merely a box to tick or a formality to fulfill—it is the cornerstone of long-term viability, competitiveness, and stakeholder trust. As businesses strive to carve out their path amidst complexity and ambiguity, those who master the art of risk management will undoubtedly emerge as leaders, charting a course toward a future defined by resilience, prosperity, and enduring success.

CHAPTER 6:
Understanding the Difference Between Cash and Profit

"Entrepreneurs` believe that profit is what matters most in a new enterprise. But profit is secondary. Cash flow matters most."

PETER DRUCKER

IN THE WORLD OF BUSINESS, the terms "cash" and "profit" are often used interchangeably, leading to confusion among entrepreneurs and managers. However, understanding the fundamental difference between these two concepts is crucial for making informed financial decisions and ensuring the long-term success of any enterprise.

Cash embodies immediate liquidity essential for day-to-day operations, while profit reflects the surplus gained from revenue after deducting expenses. Understanding this duality empowers stakeholders to navigate financial challenges, capitalize on opportunities effectively and avoid misunderstanding between business and personal funds.

THE CONCEPT OF CASH

Cash is the lifeblood of any business. It refers to the actual physical currency, as well as funds in bank accounts that can be readily accessed and used for transactions. Cash includes not only money received from sales but also any loans or investments that have been converted into cash and are available for immediate use.

Cash flow is the movement of cash in and out of a business over a specific period, typically a month, quarter, or year. Positive cash flow occurs when the cash inflows exceed outflows, while negative cash flow indicates that a business is spending more cash than it is generating. Cash flow is essential for meeting short-term obligations such as payroll, rent, utilities, and supplier payments.

Having said that, a common question that arises is: How much cash surplus should be kept?

It is not an exact answer but, the ideal cash flow surplus for a company can vary widely depending on factors such as industry, business model, growth stage, economic conditions, and specific financial goals. However, a common benchmark for assessing cash flow health is the cash flow coverage ratio, which measures the ability of a company to meet its financial obligations with its operating cash flow.

A good suggestion is to keep a cash flow surplus of around 10% to 20% of revenues, so it can provide a comfortable buffer for a company to cover unexpected expenses, invest in growth opportunities, and weather economic downturns.

It is important for companies to assess their cash flow needs based on their individual circumstances, including factors such as debt obligations, capital expenditure requirements, working capital needs, and potential future investments. Additionally, maintaining a balance between reinvesting cash into the business for growth and having a sufficient surplus for stability and resilience is key. The ideal cash flow surplus percentage will depend on the unique characteristics and goals of each company.

THE CONCEPT OF PROFIT

Profit, on the other hand, is a measure of a company's financial performance over a specific period, typically a month, quarter, or year. It is calculated by subtracting total expenses from total revenue. Profit can be further categorized into gross profit, operating profit, and net profit, each providing insights into various aspects of a company's operations.

- Gross profit represents the difference between revenue and the cost of goods sold (COGS). It reflects the profitability of a company's core business activities and is a key indicator of operational efficiency.

- Operating profit is derived by subtracting operating expenses (e.g., salaries, rent, utilities, and marketing) from gross profit. It measures the profitability of a company's regular business operations, excluding non-operating income and expenses.

- Net profit, also known as the bottom line, is the amount remaining after deducting all expenses, including taxes and interest, from total revenue. Net profit is the ultimate measure of a company's profitability and indicates how much money is left for shareholders after all expenses have been paid.

KEY DIFFERENCES BETWEEN CASH AND PROFIT

While cash and profit are both essential financial metrics, they represent various aspects of a business's financial health and performance. Understanding the distinctions between cash and profit is crucial for effective financial management and decision-making.

1. **Timing:** Cash transactions impact cash flow immediately, whereas profit is recognized over time as revenues are earned and expenses are incurred.

2. **Accrual Basis *vs.* Cash Basis**: Profit is typically calculated on an accrual basis, which recognizes revenue when it is earned and expenses when they are incurred, regardless of when cash actually changes hands. In contrast, cash flow is calculated on a cash basis, recording transactions only when cash is received or paid out.

3. **Non-Cash Items:** Profit may include non-cash items such as depreciation, amortization, and non-cash expenses, which do not affect cash flow. Conversely, cash flow does not account for non-cash items and focuses solely on actual cash transactions.

4. **Long-Term Viability:** While profit is important for measuring overall profitability and growth potential, cash flow is critical for ensuring short-term liquidity and the ability to meet immediate financial obligations.

IMPORTANCE OF BALANCING CASH AND PROFIT

Although cash and profit are distinct concepts, they are interconnected and complementary aspects of a business's financial performance. While profitability is essential for long-term sustainability and growth, adequate cash flow is necessary to support day-to-day operations and prevent liquidity crises.

Striking the right balance between cash and profit requires careful financial planning, effective budgeting, and proactive management of both revenue and expenses. By understanding the difference between cash and profit and monitoring both metrics regularly, businesses can optimize their financial performance, mitigate risks, and achieve sustainable growth in the long run.

CONCLUSION

Knowing the difference between cash and profit can make all the difference. Cash is the money you have right now, while profit looks at the bigger picture over time. Both are essential for running a successful business.

Misinterpreting the distinction between cash and profit could lead to a significant misunderstanding for business owners: the crucial need to separate personal and business finances. Blurring these lines may result in various complications and pose risks to the stability and expansion of the enterprise.

The distinction between personal and business funds is not merely a matter of financial tidiness; it is a fundamental safeguard for the integrity of the business. By keeping personal finances separate, owners ensure transparency, accuracy, and accountability in their financial records. This clarity is indispensable for making informed decisions, accurately assessing the financial health of the business, and complying with regulatory requirements.

Furthermore, mixing personal and business finances can obscure the true profitability and performance of the enterprise. It blurs the lines between personal income and business revenue, making it challenging to measure the business's actual financial standing and impeding strategic planning.

Moreover, commingling funds exposes the business to heightened risks, including legal liabilities and tax complications. In the event of an audit or legal dispute, the lack of separation between personal and business finances can result in legal ramifications, financial penalties, and reputational damage.

Beyond the logistical and legal ramifications, mixing personal and business funds can undermine the professionalism and credibility of the business. It sends a signal of financial irresponsibility and may deter potential investors, creditors, and partners from engaging with the enterprise.

The importance of maintaining a clear delineation between personal and business finances cannot be overstated. It is a fundamental practice that underpins the financial integrity, stability, and growth of the business. I constantly advise clients that owners who uphold this principle demonstrate a commitment to sound financial management, mitigate risks, and position their enterprises for long-term success.

So, the next time you are thinking about your business's finances, remember that cash is about what is happening right now, while profit is about the bigger picture. By understanding both, you will be better equipped to make smart decisions and keep your business thriving.

CHAPTER 7:
The Fundamental Role of Accounting in Business Finance

"You have to know accounting. It is the language of practical business life. It was a very useful thing to deliver to civilization. I have heard it came to civilization through Venice which of course was once the great commercial power in the Mediterranean. However, double entry bookkeeping was a hell of an invention."

CHARLIE MUNGER

IN BUSINESS FINANCE, WHERE DECISIONS are made with an eye toward optimizing value and managing risk, accounting serves as the cornerstone upon which all strategies and actions are built.

In this chapter, we will discuss the indispensable role that accounting plays in business finance and explore its significance in decision-making processes.

Accounting serves as the foundation of business finance, encompassing both **bookkeeping** and **the accounting cycle**.

Bookkeeping: Bookkeeping is the process of recording financial transactions in an organized and systematic manner. It involves keeping track of all monetary transactions, including purchases, sales, receipts, and payments. The primary objective of bookkeeping is to maintain accurate and up-to-date financial records that reflect the financial activities of a business entity.

In bookkeeping, transactions are recorded in journals, which are then summarized and posted to ledger accounts. The ledger accounts are classified into various categories, such as assets, liabilities, equity, revenue, and expenses. This classification enables businesses to track their financial performance and comply with accounting principles and standards.

Bookkeeping lays the foundation for the accounting cycle by providing the raw data necessary for financial analysis, reporting, and decision-making. Without accurate and reliable bookkeeping records, it would be challenging for businesses to assess their financial position, measure profitability, and make informed decisions.

The Accounting Cycle: The accounting cycle is a series of sequential steps that businesses follow to process financial transactions and produce financial statements. It involves several stages, including:

1. **Identifying Transactions:** The accounting cycle begins with the identification of financial transactions that occur within the business. These transactions may include sales, purchases, investments, borrowings, and expenses.

2. **Recording Transactions:** Once the transactions are identified, they are recorded in the appropriate journals based on the type of transaction. For example, sales transactions

are recorded in the sales journal, while purchase transactions are recorded in the purchase journal.

3. **Posting to Ledger:** After recording transactions in the journals, the next step is to post them to ledger accounts. Each transaction is posted to the respective ledger account, maintaining the balance of each account.

4. **Adjusting Entries:** At the end of the accounting period, adjusting entries are made to ensure that the financial statements reflect the true financial position of the business. These entries are necessary to account for accrued expenses, prepaid expenses, unearned revenue, depreciation, and other adjustments.

5. **Preparing Financial Statements:** Once all adjusting entries are made, financial statements are prepared. The primary financial statements include the income statement, balance sheet, and cash flow statement. These statements provide a summary of the business's financial performance, financial position, and cash flows.

6. **Closing Entries:** After the financial statements are prepared, closing entries are made to close temporary accounts such as revenue and expense accounts. This process resets the accounts for the next accounting period.

7. **Post-Closing Trial Balance:** A post-closing trial balance is prepared to ensure that the accounting records are in balance after closing entries are made.

The accounting cycle repeats itself for each accounting period, typically on a monthly, quarterly, or annual basis, depending on the reporting business's requirements.

Bookkeeping and the accounting cycle are essential components of business finance, providing the framework for recording, processing, and reporting financial transactions. By maintaining accurate records and following the accounting cycle, businesses can ensure compliance with accounting standards, assess their financial performance, and make informed decisions to drive growth and profitability.

Accounting is not merely about recording financial transactions; it is the language of business, providing a systematic framework for interpreting, analyzing, and communicating financial information.

UNDERSTANDING FINANCIAL PERFORMANCE THOUGHT ACCOUNTING

Accounting provides a comprehensive view of a company's financial performance, allowing stakeholders to assess its profitability, liquidity, solvency, and efficiency.

Through financial statements such as the income statement, balance sheet, and cash flow statement, managers, investors, creditors, and regulators gain insights into the company's past performance and its potential for future growth.

These statements serve as vital tools for evaluating the effectiveness of business operations, identifying areas for improvement, and making informed decisions.

DECISION-MAKING STARTS USING ACCOUNTING

Effective decision-making in business finance hinges on accurate and reliable financial information. Whether it involves capital budgeting, investment analysis, or strategic planning, accounting data serves as the bedrock upon which decisions are made.

For instance, when evaluating investment opportunities, managers rely on financial metrics such as net present value (NPV), internal rate of return (IRR), and return on investment (ROI) derived from accounting data to assess the feasibility and profitability of projects.

Similarly, creditors use financial ratios and performance indicators derived from accounting information to evaluate a company's creditworthiness and determine lending terms.

ENSURING COMPLIANCE AND TRANSPARENCY WITH ACCOUNTING

In an increasingly complex regulatory environment, adherence to accounting standards and principles is paramount for corporate governance and regulatory compliance.

Accounting standards such as Generally Accepted Accounting Principles (GAAP) and International Financial Reporting Standards (IFRS) provide a common framework for preparing financial statements, ensuring consistency, comparability, and transparency across different entities.

Compliance with these standards not only enhances the credibility of financial reporting but also fosters trust among investors, creditors, and other stakeholders.

ASSESSING RISK AND PERFORMANCE

Accounting plays a crucial role in assessing and managing risk in business finance. By accurately measuring and reporting financial performance, accounting enables stakeholders to identify potential risks and vulnerabilities early on.

Through techniques such as financial statement analysis, trend analysis, and ratio analysis, managers can gauge the financial health of the company, identify red flags, and take measures to mitigate risks.

Moreover, accounting data serves as a basis for risk assessment models and stress testing scenarios, enabling companies to evaluate the potential impact of various risk factors on their financial stability and resilience.

FACILITATING COMMUNICATION AND STAKEHOLDER ENGAGEMENT

Accounting serves as a universal language that facilitates communication and collaboration among various stakeholders in business finance.

Whether it is communicating financial results to investors, negotiating lending terms with creditors, or reporting compliance with regulatory requirements, accounting provides a standardized framework for conveying complex financial information in a clear, concise, and meaningful manner.

Effective communication fosters trust, enhances transparency, and strengthens relationships with stakeholders, contributing to the long-term success and sustainability of the company.

CONCLUSION

In summary, accounting serves as the fundamental framework for business financial management. It provides a comprehensive toolkit comprising various methodologies and techniques essential for not just assessing financial performance but also for guiding strategic decision-making, ensuring regulatory compliance, managing risk effectively, and fostering robust communication channels among stakeholders.

By embracing the principles of accounting and harnessing financial information intelligently, companies can navigate the challenges present in today's dynamic business environment. Accounting enables organizations to gain valuable insights into their financial standing, identify areas of strength and weakness, and make informed decisions to steer the company toward sustainable growth and profitability.

Moreover, accounting is not merely about crunching numbers; it is about translating complex financial data into meaningful insights that drive strategic action. By leveraging accounting principles effectively, companies can identify emerging trends, anticipate market shifts, and seize opportunities for expansion, thus positioning themselves as agile and forward-thinking entities in the competitive landscape.

Furthermore, accounting plays a crucial role in fostering transparency and accountability, both internally and externally. By maintaining accurate financial records and adhering to regulatory standards, organizations can build trust and credibility among investors, creditors, and other stakeholders, thereby enhancing their reputation and long-term viability in the market.

Accounting is not just a technical discipline; it is a strategic imperative for businesses seeking to thrive in an increasingly complex and interconnected global economy.

By embracing the principles of accounting and leveraging financial information effectively, companies can unlock new pathways to growth, create lasting value for their shareholders and stakeholders, and establish themselves as leaders in their respective industries.

CHAPTER 8:
Financial Statements - The Bedrock of Financial Management

"Know what you own, and know why you own it."

PETER LYNCH

I N THE WORLD OF FINANCE, being able to understand and analyze financial statements is indispensable.

Whether you are a seasoned investor, an emerging entrepreneur, or a business executive, a firm grasp of financial statements is essential for making informed decisions and managing resources effectively.

In this chapter, we will delve into three fundamental financial statements: the Balance Sheet, the Profit and Loss Statement (P&L), and the Statement of Cash Flows. We will explore their significance, their interconnections, and how they serve as invaluable tools for financial management.

THE BALANCE SHEET: UNDERSTANDING FINANCIAL POSITIONS

The Balance Sheet is a company's financial position snapshot at a specific point in time. It presents the company's assets, liabilities, and equity, providing a clear picture of what the company owns and owes, as well as the shareholders' stake in the company.

Components of a Balance Sheet:

- **Assets:** These are resources owned by the company, which can be tangible (such as cash, inventory, and property) or intangible (such as patents and trademarks).

- **Liabilities:** These represent the company's obligations or debts to external parties, including creditors and suppliers.

- **Equity:** Equity represents the ownership interest in the company held by shareholders. It is calculated as the residual interest after deducting liabilities from assets.

Importance of the Balance Sheet:

- **Financial Health Assessment:** The Balance Sheet provides insights into a company's financial health and stability. By analyzing the relationship between assets, liabilities, and equity, stakeholders can assess solvency and liquidity.

- **Basis for Decision Making:** Investors, creditors, and management rely on the Balance Sheet to evaluate investment opportunities, assess creditworthiness, and make strategic decisions.

- **Comparison and Benchmarking:** It facilitates comparison with competitors and industry benchmarks, aiding in identifying strengths, weaknesses, and areas for improvement.

THE PROFIT AND LOSS STATEMENT (P&L): EVALUATING PERFORMANCE

The Profit and Loss Statement, also known as the Income Statement, is a financial statement that shows a company's revenues, expenses, and profits over a specific period, typically monthly, quarterly, or yearly.

Components of a P&L Statement:

- **Revenue:** This represents the income generated from the company's primary operations.

- **Expenses:** Expenses are the costs incurred by the company in conducting its business activities. They can include operating expenses, interest payments, and taxes.

- **Net Income:** Net income, also referred to as the bottom line, is the difference between total revenue and total expenses. It indicates the company's profitability during the period.

Importance of the P&L Statement:

- **Performance Evaluation:** The P&L Statement provides a comprehensive view of a company's operational performance and profitability. It helps stakeholders gauge efficiency, identify trends, and track growth over time.

- **Decision Making**: Management relies on the P&L Statement to make strategic decisions, such as pricing strategies, cost-cutting initiatives, and investment prioritization.

- **Investor Confidence:** Investors and analysts use the P&L Statement to assess the company's financial health, growth potential, and ability to generate returns.

STATEMENT OF CASH FLOWS: TRACKING CASH MOVEMENT

The Statement of Cash Flows is a financial statement that shows the inflow and outflow of cash from operating, investing, and financing activities over a specific period. With this statement, it is possible to track a company's liquidity, cash position, and ability to meet financial obligations.

Components of a Cash Flow Statement:

- **Operating Activities:** Cash flows from operating activities include cash receipts and payments related to the company's primary business operations, such as sales, purchases, and expenses.

- **Investing Activities:** Investing activities involve cash flows from the buying and selling of long-term assets, such as property, plants, and equipment, as well as investments in securities.

- **Financing Activities:** Cash flows from financing activities include transactions related to raising capital and repaying debts, such as issuing stocks, borrowing loans, and paying dividends.

Importance of the Cash Flow Statement:

- **Liquidity Management:** The Cash Flow Statement helps management assess the company's liquidity position and its ability to generate sufficient cash to meet short-term obligations.

- **Investment Analysis:** Investors use the Cash Flow Statement to evaluate the quality of earnings and assess the sustainability of cash flows, which can differ from reported profits due to non-cash items.

- **Risk Assessment:** Creditors and stakeholders analyze cash flow patterns to gauge the company's financial stability, debt repayment capacity, and susceptibility to financial distress.

INTERCONNECTIONS AND ANALYSIS:

While each financial statement provides valuable insights on its own, their true power lies in their interconnections and the holistic analysis they enable. For instance:

- **Leverage Analysis:** By comparing data from the Balance Sheet and the P&L Statement, stakeholders can assess the company's leverage ratio, debt-to-equity ratio, and interest coverage ratio, which are critical indicators of financial risk.

- **Working Capital Management:** The interplay between the Balance Sheet and the Cash Flow Statement aids in evaluating working capital efficiency, liquidity trends, and cash conversion cycles.

- **Valuation Metrics:** Integrated analysis of all three statements helps in estimating key valuation metrics, such as price-to-earnings ratio (P/E), price-to-book ratio (P/B), and free cash flow yield, guiding investment decisions.

CONCLUSION

In conclusion, the Balance Sheet, the Profit and Loss Statement, and the Statement of Cash Flows serve as indispensable tools for financial management. By understanding their components, significance, and interrelationships, stakeholders can make informed decisions, mitigate risks, and drive sustainable growth.

Mastery of financial statements is not merely a skill; it is the cornerstone of effective financial management in today's dynamic business landscape.

It becomes unmistakably clear that the Balance Sheet, the Profit and Loss Statement, and the Statement of Cash Flows are not just documents; they are essential tools that drive effective financial management within organizations. These financial statements provide invaluable insights into the financial health, performance, and liquidity of a business, enabling stakeholders to make well-informed decisions that steer the company toward success.

By diving into the components, significance, and interplay of these financial statements, stakeholders gain a comprehensive understanding of the organization's financial position and trajectory.

The Balance Sheet reveals the company's assets, liabilities, and equity at a given point in time, offering a snapshot of its financial health and stability. Meanwhile, the Profit and Loss Statement delineates revenues, expenses, and profitability over a specific period, shedding light on the company's operational efficiency and revenue-generating capabilities. Lastly, the Statement of Cash Flows shows the inflows and outflows of cash during the reporting period, providing crucial insights into the company's liquidity and ability to meet its financial obligations.

By comprehending these financial statements, stakeholders can effectively assess the risks and opportunities inherent in the business environment. Armed with this knowledge, they can make strategic decisions to optimize resource allocation, mitigate financial risks, and capitalize on growth opportunities.

Whether it is identifying areas for cost reduction, evaluating investment opportunities, or formulating strategic expansion plans, mastery of financial statements empowers stakeholders to navigate the complexities of the business landscape with confidence and clarity.

Moreover, in today's fast-paced and competitive business environment, where uncertainties abound and market dynamics evolve rapidly, the importance of financial knowledge cannot be overstated.

Mastery of financial statements is not just a skill; it is the foundation of effective financial management that drives sustainable growth and long-term success. By fostering a culture of financial literacy and proficiency within organizations, stakeholders can cultivate resilience, adaptability, and agility, positioning the company for continued prosperity and resilience amidst the ever-changing business landscape.

CHAPTER 9:

Why Getting Help from
Experts Matters

"One of the biggest defects in life is the inability to ask for help."

ROBERT KIYOSAKI

Operating a business entails navigating numerous financial challenges, from regulatory compliance to strategic investments and risk management.

Fortunately, there are skilled professionals who specialize in these areas, forming the basis of financial expertise. Among them are accountants, business financial advisors, and business mentors.

In this chapter, we will underscore the significance of surrounding yourself and your business with these professionals, who can provide invaluable assistance and guidance in overcoming financial hurdles.

KEEPING THINGS STRAIGHT WITH ACCOUNTANTS

In the world of business, where every dollar counts, accountants are like financial superheroes. They work behind the scenes to make sure all your money records are correct and follow the rules. This helps you make smart decisions and keeps everyone trusting your business.

There are many rules about finances in business, like how to report your finances and pay taxes. Accountants are experts in these rules. They help you understand and follow them, so you do not get into trouble with the government or make mistakes that could hurt your business.

Imagine if your bank statement did not match what you think you spent. Accountants make sure all the money coming in and going out of your business is recorded accurately. They check everything carefully, so you can trust your financial reports to show the true picture of how your business is doing.

When your financial reports are accurate and reliable, people trust your business more. Whether it is your investors, customers, or the government, they need to know they can rely on your numbers. Accountants help you build this trust by making sure your financial reports are clear and honest.

Accountants are like financial guardians for your business. They make sure your money records are correct and follow the rules. This helps you make better decisions and builds trust with everyone involved in your business. So, it is important to appreciate their hard work in keeping your finances in order.

MAKING SMART MOVES WITH BUSINESS FINANCIAL ADVISORS

Business financial advisors are like expert guides who help businesses navigate the complex world of finance. They provide invaluable advice and support to ensure that companies make smart decisions about their finances.

First, business financial advisors take the time to understand the unique goals and objectives of your company. Whether it is expanding into new markets, increasing profitability, or managing cash flow effectively, they work closely with you to develop a clear financial strategy that aligns with your business goals.

They are experts in financial management, with a deep understanding of various financial concepts and strategies. They can help you analyze your company's financial health, identify areas for improvement, and develop action plans to optimize financial performance. From budgeting and forecasting to financial reporting and analysis, their expertise covers all aspects of business finance.

Investing wisely is crucial for the long-term success of any business. Business financial advisors provide strategic guidance on investment decisions, helping you evaluate potential opportunities and risks. Whether it is investing in innovative technology, expanding operations, or acquiring other companies, they help you make informed decisions that maximize returns and minimize risks.

Every business face risks, from economic downturns to regulatory changes and unexpected events. They help you identify and manage these risks effectively. They can develop risk management strategies, such as insurance policies, hedging techniques, and contingency plans, to protect your company's assets and ensure its long-term viability.

Compliance with financial regulations and governance standards is essential for maintaining the trust of stakeholders and safeguarding your company's reputation.

Business financial advisors help ensure that your company adheres to all relevant regulations and standards. They can conduct audits, review financial processes, and implement internal controls to ensure compliance and mitigate the risk of financial misconduct.

In addition to their technical expertise, business financial advisors provide valuable strategic insights to help you make sound business decisions. They can offer perspectives on market trends, industry benchmarks, and competitive analysis, enabling you to identify opportunities for growth and stay ahead of the competition.

In summary, business financial advisors play a crucial role in helping businesses make smart financial moves. From developing strategic financial plans to managing investments, mitigating risks, and ensuring compliance, they provide guidance and support that can make a significant difference in the success and sustainability of your company.

By partnering with them, businesses can navigate the complexities of the financial landscape with confidence and achieve their long-term goals.

LEARNING FROM BUSINESS MENTORS: THE POWER OF LEARNING FROM BUSINESS MENTORS

Business mentors are like experienced guides who offer invaluable insights and guidance to individuals seeking to navigate the complexities of entrepreneurship and business management. Their wealth of knowledge and firsthand experience make them invaluable resources for those looking to learn and grow in their professional endeavors.

One of the most significant advantages of learning from business mentors is the opportunity to tap into their wealth of experience. Mentors have often faced similar challenges and obstacles in their own entrepreneurial journey and have learned valuable lessons along the way. By sharing their experiences, both successes and failures, mentors provide invaluable wisdom that can help mentees avoid common pitfalls and make informed decisions in their own ventures.

Business mentors offer guidance and support in strategic decision-making, helping mentees navigate complex business scenarios with confidence and clarity. Whether it is developing a business plan, expanding into new markets, or negotiating partnerships, mentors provide valuable perspectives and insights that can inform and shape strategic initiatives. Their guidance is grounded in real-world experience, offering practical advice that is tailored to the specific needs and goals of the mentee.

Beyond business strategy, mentors also play a crucial role in fostering personal and professional development. They serve as trusted advisors and confidants, offering mentorship and support in areas such as leadership development, communication skills, and goal-setting. Mentors provide encouragement, accountability, and constructive feedback, helping mentees unlock their full potential and achieve their professional aspirations.

In addition to their wealth of knowledge and experience, mentors often have extensive networks and connections within their industry or field of expertise. By learning from a mentor, mentees gain access to valuable networking opportunities and the chance to forge meaningful relationships with other professionals and industry leaders. These connections can open doors to new opportunities, partnerships, and collaborations that can accelerate the mentee's career or business growth.

The relationship between a mentor and mentee is often characterized by long-term support and guidance. Mentors are committed to the success and growth of their mentees and are willing to invest their time, energy, and expertise to help them achieve their goals. Whether it is providing ongoing advice, serving as a sounding board for ideas, or offering encouragement during challenging times, mentors play a crucial role in the continued development and success of their mentees.

Learning from business mentors is a valuable and transformative experience for individuals seeking to excel in the world of entrepreneurship and business management.

Mentors offer a wealth of experience, guidance, and support that can help mentees navigate challenges, make informed decisions, and achieve their professional goals.

By embracing the wisdom and guidance of mentors, individuals can accelerate their learning and development, unlocking new opportunities for growth and success in their entrepreneurial journey.

WHY IT ALL MATTERS: SETTING YOUR BUSINESS UP FOR SUCCESS

Seeking help from experts such as accountants, financial advisors, and business mentors is not just about ticking boxes or following rules. It is about laying a solid foundation for the success and sustainability of your business. Here is why it matters:

1. **Informed Decision-Making:** With the guidance of experts, you gain access to insights and perspectives that can help you make better decisions for your business. Whether it is financial planning, investment strategies, or strategic direction, their expertise allows you to weigh options, anticipate outcomes, and choose the path that aligns with your goals and vision.

2. **Growth and Expansion:** Experts can help you identify opportunities for growth and expansion that you may not have considered on your own. Whether it is optimizing your finances, exploring new markets, or expanding your product/service offerings, their guidance can help you capitalize on opportunities and take your business to the next level.

3. **Mitigating Risks:** Running a business comes with inherent risks, from economic downturns to industry disruptions and regulatory changes. Experts can help you identify and mitigate these risks effectively. Whether it is through risk management strategies, contingency planning, or compliance measures, their expertise can help safeguard your business against potential threats and uncertainties.

4. **Building Credibility and Trust:** When you work with experts, you signal to stakeholders—whether they are investors, customers, or regulatory bodies—that you take your business seriously. By ensuring accuracy,

transparency, and compliance in your financial practices, you build credibility and trust, which are essential for fostering positive relationships and securing support for your business endeavors.

5. **Being Prepared for Challenges:** No business journey is without its challenges. However, with the guidance of experts, you can be better prepared to navigate these challenges when they arise. Whether it is financial set-backs, market fluctuations, or unexpected obstacles, their support and advice can help you weather the storm and emerge stronger on the other side.

CONCLUSION

Seeking help from experts is not just a formality; it is a strategic investment in the success and resilience of your business. Moreover, leveraging the expertise of these professionals enables you to navigate the complex terrain of business with confidence and clarity. Their mentorship empowers you to identify and mitigate potential risks effectively while also bolstering the credibility of your enterprise.

The objective extends far beyond short-term gains; it is about positioning your business for sustained success and resilience amidst the ever-evolving landscape of commerce. With the support and guidance of experts, you lay a sturdy groundwork that paves the way for enduring prosperity and relevance in today's dynamic business environment.

CHAPTER 10:

Embracing Technological Advancements in Financial Management and Accounting

"Innovation distinguishes between a leader and a follower."

STEVE JOBS

THE INTEGRATION OF TECHNOLOGY HAS revolutionized the way businesses and individuals manage their finances; that is a fact. No longer confined to the realms of large corporations, the transformative power of digital tools has permeated every facet of modern commerce, from fledgling startups to seasoned enterprises.

This chapter explores the profound impact of technology on financial management, delving into its pivotal role in enhancing operational efficiency, ensuring precision in accounting practices, and empowering stakeholders to make informed, strategic decisions.

As we navigate through the intricate interplay of innovation and finance, it becomes increasingly evident that embracing technological advancements is not merely an option but an imperative for businesses and individuals alike striving for sustainable growth and prosperity.

THE RISE OF FINANCIAL TECHNOLOGY (FINTECH)

The emergence of Fintech has reshaped the landscape of financial management and accounting. Fintech encompasses a wide array of technological innovations, including cloud computing, artificial intelligence (AI), and data analytics. These advancements have democratized access to financial services, enabling users to seamlessly conduct transactions, monitor investments, and optimize cash flow.

For example, online grocery shopping platforms, like Instacart, utilize AI algorithms to streamline the shopping experience for consumers. These platforms analyze users' shopping preferences, dietary restrictions, and purchasing habits to suggest personalized grocery lists. By automating the shopping process, online grocery platforms offer convenient and time-saving solutions for individuals looking to stock up on essentials without the hassle of visiting physical stores.

STREAMLINING FINANCIAL PROCESSES WITH SOFTWARE SOLUTIONS

Gone are the days of cumbersome spreadsheets and manual data entry. Today, there are software solutions to the diverse needs of financial management and accounting. From popular platforms like QuickBooks and Xero for bookkeeping to advanced enterprise resource planning (ERP) systems such as SAP and Oracle, organizations have a multitude of options to automate routine tasks, reconcile accounts, and generate comprehensive financial reports in real-time.

An illustration of this is cloud-based accounting software, which is extensively utilized by small enterprises and freelancers to oversee their finances. QuickBooks and Xero, among others, are prime examples, offering a range of features such as invoicing, expense tracking, and financial reporting. Theirs streamlines accounting tasks and grants users access to financial data from any location at any time. Their integration with third-party applications enhances functionality, enabling users to optimize workflows and tailor their accounting practices to suit their requirements.

HARNESSING THE POWER OF ARTIFICIAL INTELLIGENCE AND MACHINE LEARNING

Artificial intelligence (AI) and machine learning algorithms have empowered financial professionals to extract actionable insights from vast datasets with unparalleled speed and accuracy. These technologies enable predictive analytics, fraud detection, and risk management, thereby enhancing decision-making processes and mitigating potential financial pitfalls.

As an example, traditional credit scoring models rely on historical credit data to assess borrowers' creditworthiness. AI-powered credit scoring models, such as those developed by companies like NovaScore, leverage machine learning algorithms to analyze alternative data sources and predict credit risk more accurately. By incorporating factors like employment history, education level, and social media behavior, these models enable lenders to extend credit to underserved populations while minimizing default risks.

LEVERAGING CLOUD-BASED PLATFORMS FOR COLLABORATIVE FINANCIAL MANAGEMENT

Cloud computing has transformed the way teams collaborate on financial tasks, irrespective of geographical constraints. Cloud-based platforms like Google Workspace, Microsoft 365, and Dropbox facilitate seamless document sharing, real-time collaboration, and secure data storage. This level of accessibility fosters greater transparency and efficiency in financial operations, enabling stakeholders to monitor progress, track expenses, and collaborate on budgets effortlessly.

Google Sheets, as an example and a part of Google Workspace, offers a collaborative and cloud-based alternative to traditional spreadsheet software like Microsoft Excel. Multiple users can work on the same spreadsheet simultaneously, making it ideal for collaborative financial planning and budgeting. Integration with other Google Workspace apps, such as Google Docs and Google Drive, further enhances productivity by centralizing documents and enabling real-time communication among team members.

NAVIGATING REGULATORY COMPLIANCE WITH TECH-DRIVEN SOLUTIONS

In an increasingly stringent regulatory environment, compliance with financial regulations is essential. Tech-driven solutions, such as regulatory compliance software and automated reporting tools, help organizations navigate complex regulatory frameworks efficiently.

Examples of tax compliance software, such as Avalara and Vertex, automate the calculation, filing, and reporting of taxes to ensure compliance with local, state, and federal regulations. These platforms integrate with accounting systems to streamline tax-related processes, minimize errors, and generate accurate tax returns. Additionally, they provide updates on changes in tax laws and regulations, enabling businesses to adapt their tax strategies accordingly and avoid costly penalties.

CONCLUSION

It is becoming increasingly clear that embracing innovative ideas and ways of doing things is not just helpful—it is necessary if you want to do well financially in today's changing world. By using innovative technology in smart ways, both people and businesses can make their work smoother, make better decisions, and keep their efforts for growth going strong.

Embracing innovative ideas is not just about using the newest gadgets or software. It is about creating a culture where people are encouraged to think creatively, adapt to new situations, and plan ahead. People who are actively involved in trying new things are better prepared to deal with the challenges of modern markets, find new chances to succeed, and stay ahead in a competitive world.

Innovation is not just one way to be successful—it is the very foundation of how we build a better financial future.

CONCLUSION:
Embracing Financial Management

"Obstacles do not have to stop you. If you run into a wall, do not turn around and give up. Figure out how to climb it, go through it, or work around it."

MICHAEL JORDAN

I N THE DYNAMIC AND EVER-EVOLVING landscape of business finance, the ability to navigate complexities, embrace uncertainties, and capitalize on opportunities is essential for sustained success and growth.

Throughout this comprehensive exploration of business financial management, we have dived into the fundamental principles, strategies, and best practices that define effective financial decision-making, risk management, and value creation within organizations.

From the foundational concepts of financial analysis and reporting to the strategic imperatives of capital budgeting, risk management, and cash flow optimization, each chapter has offered valuable insights and actionable strategies to empower executives, managers, and financial professionals in their pursuit of financial excellence and organizational resilience.

In "**Face it!**", we have addressed key topics such as financial statement reports, cost management, capital budgeting, investment analysis, risk management, and cash flow optimization, equipping readers with the knowledge, skills, and tools necessary to navigate the complexities of business finance with confidence and clarity.

REFLECTING ON FINANCIAL MANAGEMENT PRINCIPLES

At the heart of effective business financial management lies a commitment to sound financial principles and practices that drive value creation, mitigate risks, and enhance stakeholder trust. By embracing financial transparency, accountability, and integrity, organizations can foster a culture of financial stewardship and business responsibility that resonates with investors, customers, employees, and the broader community.

Throughout this journey, we have emphasized the importance of strategic alignment, data-driven decision-making, and continuous improvement in driving organizational performance and competitiveness. By aligning financial objectives with strategic priorities, leveraging data analytics and technology to inform decision-making, and embracing a mindset of innovation and agility, companies can adapt to changing market dynamics, seize emerging opportunities, and stay ahead of the curve in today's fast-paced business environment.

EMBRACING RISK MANAGEMENT IN UNCERTAIN TIMES

In an era defined by volatility, uncertainty, and complexity, effective risk management has never been more critical. By identifying, assessing, and mitigating risks proactively, organizations can enhance resilience, protect against potential threats, and capitalize on strategic opportunities for growth and innovation.

From operational risks arising from internal processes and systems to financial risks stemming from market fluctuations and regulatory changes, "**Face it!**" has underscored the importance of a comprehensive and integrated approach to risk management. By integrating risk management into strategic planning, investment decision-making, and day-to-day operations, companies can anticipate challenges, adapt to changing circumstances, and navigate uncertainties with confidence and clarity.

MAXIMIZING VALUE THROUGH FINANCIAL DECISION-MAKING

At its core, business financial management is about maximizing value for shareholders, stakeholders, and society at large. By adopting a disciplined approach to financial decision-making, organizations can allocate resources efficiently, optimize capital investments, and create sustainable value over the long term.

Through the lens of capital budgeting, investment analysis, and cash flow optimization, "**Face it!**" has provided readers with practical information and frameworks to evaluate investment opportunities, manage cash flow effectively, and enhance financial performance. By leveraging techniques such as net present value (NPV), internal rate of return (IRR), and cash flow forecasting, companies can make informed decisions that drive profitability, growth, and shareholder wealth.

LOOKING AHEAD: NAVIGATING FUTURE CHALLENGES AND OPPORTUNITIES

As we conclude our journey through the world of business financial management, it is essential to acknowledge that the landscape continues to evolve, presenting both challenges and opportunities for organizations around the globe. From technological disruptions and regulatory changes to shifting consumer preferences and geopolitical uncertainties, the future is fraught with uncertainties that demand agility, resilience, and innovation.

In the face of these challenges, organizations must remain vigilant, adaptable, and forward-thinking in their approach to financial management. By embracing a culture of continuous learning, collaboration, and experimentation, companies can stay ahead of the curve, drive sustainable growth, and create value in an increasingly complex and interconnected world.

A commitment to financial excellence, integrity, and stewardship is essential to establishing a sound marketplace. Together, let us face the future with confidence, courage, and resilience, knowing that with the right mindset, strategies, and principles, we can overcome any challenge and seize every opportunity that comes our way.

EMBRACE IT!

This book is more than just a book on business financial management—it is a call to action, a roadmap for success, and a testament to the power of knowledge, innovation, and collaboration in driving organizational excellence. As we face the complexities of the business landscape, let us embrace the principles, strategies, and insights shared in this book to navigate challenges, seize opportunities, and chart a course toward a brighter, more prosperous future.

Dive deep into the world of business financial management and embark on a journey of discovery, growth, and transformation. Together, let us shape the future of finance and create value that transcends boundaries, enriches lives, and leaves a lasting legacy for generations to come. Let us roll up the sleeves and **FACE IT!**

ACKNOWLEDGEMENTS

I N THE JOURNEY OF WRITING this book, I have been blessed with the support, encouragement, and inspiration of many individuals who have played pivotal roles in its creation.

First, I want to express my heartfelt appreciation to my parents, Talito and Doracila. Your unwavering belief in me and your endless support have been essential to my achievements in life. Thank you for instilling in me the values of hard work, perseverance, and determination.

To my beloved spouse, Fernanda, and our beautiful daughters, Bruna and Gabriela, your love, understanding, and patience have been my source of strength throughout this journey. Your unwavering support has made it possible for me to pursue my passion and complete this project. I am forever grateful for your presence in my life.

I am also deeply grateful to my dear friends, whose encouragement and support have been invaluable. Your belief in my abilities has been a constant source of motivation, and I am thankful for your unwavering friendship.

Throughout my career, I've had the privilege of collaborating with clients and colleagues whose trust and confidence in my abilities have propelled me forward in my professional journey. To each of you, I extend my gratitude.

Finally, and above all, I want to acknowledge the divine guidance and grace of God. In moments of doubt and uncertainty, it is Your strength that has sustained me. Your blessings have been abundant, and I am humbled by Your presence in my life. All praise to my Lord and Savior, Jesus Christ.

To all those mentioned above and to the countless others who have contributed in ways big and small, thank you for being a part of this journey. This book would not have been possible without your support, and for that, I am grateful.

With heartfelt appreciation,

SANDRO ENDLER